YOU M... ...R THIS

1936

MILESTONES, MEMORIES,
TRIVIA AND FACTS, NEWS EVENTS,
PROMINENT PERSONALITIES &
SPORTS HIGHLIGHTS OF THE YEAR

TO :

FROM :

MESSAGE :

*selected and researched
by
betsy dexter*

WARNER  TREASURES ™

PUBLISHED BY WARNER BOOKS

A TIME WARNER COMPANY

Warner Books, Inc.
1271 Avenue of the Americas
New York, New York 10020

Warner Treasures is a
trademark of Warner Books, Inc.

A Time Warner Company

DESIGN:
CAROL BOKUNIEWICZ DESIGN
PRINTED IN SINGAPORE
FIRST PRINTING: SEPTEMBER 1996
10 9 8 7 6 5 4 3 2 1
ISBN: 0-446-91149-6

It was the year **FRANKLIN DELANO ROOSEVELT** was reelected by a landslide, defeating Alfred M. Landon in the greatest outpouring of voters in the nation's history.

newsreel

A HEAT WAVE THAT BROILED THE NATION IN JULY KILLED 3,000.

'36

Returns showed that the president received 523 electoral votes, to a paltry 8 for his Republican opponent. Every state but Vermont and Maine went with Roosevelt. The election proved an overwhelming endorsement of the New Deal, the bold initiative that sought to boost the nation out of the Depression. Vast numbers of workers and unemployed trekked to the polls, a large portion of them for the first time. Kansas Governor Landon attacked Roosevelt viciously throughout the campaign, accusing him of acting like a dictator.

Floods swept 12 midwest states; 134 died, and 20,000 were left homeless.

CONGRESS PASSED THE **WALSH-HEALEY (PUBLIC CONTRACTS) ACT,** SETTING MINIMUM EMPLOYEE WAGES FOR COMPANIES WITH GOVERNMENT CONTRACTS. EIGHT-HOUR DAYS, 40-HOUR WEEKS, AND A BAN ON CHILD LABOR WERE ENFORCED.

THE BURLINGTON RAILROAD's DENVER ZEPHYR set a world's long-distance speed record for trains. It made a Chicago to Denver run in just over 12 hours and 12 minutes, at an average speed of 83.3 miles per hour.

BOULDER DAM was completed on the Colorado River, on the Nevada and Arizona border. The dam created Lake Mead, America's largest artificial lake, with a capacity of more than 10 trillion gallons. The dam was the highest in the world.

MANY AMERICANS RUSHED TO SPAIN TO FIGHT ALONGSIDE SPANISH LOYALISTS AGAINST THE FASCISTS.

Charles "Lucky" Luciano

On June 18, **charles "lucky" luciano** was found guilty on 62 counts of compulsory prostitution. The mobster ran a $12 million a year prostitution ring in New York City.

Edward with Wallis Simpson

edward viii became King of England but abdicated after the British government opposed his marriage to Wallis Warfield Simpson. George VI, brother of Edward, became king, ending the most profound constitutional crisis in modern English history.

international

headlines

In the Middle East, Saudi Arabia and Iraq signed a treaty of nonaggression. The Arab High Committee was formed, formalizing opposition to Jewish claims in Palestine.

IN NICARAGUA, ANASTASIO SOMOZA SEIZED POWER AFTER A SUCCESSFUL COUP AGAINST THE REIGNING LIBERAL REGIME.

Giant hailstones killed 19 people in South Africa.

Hitler   *Mussolini*

Hitler and Mussolini signed an accord known as the **"ROME-BERLIN AXIS,"** a declaration of mutual support.

FLASH! CHINA BOASTED THE WORLD'S LARGEST POPULATION, 422 MILLION. INDIA HAD 360 MILLION. USSR, 173 MILLION. JAPAN, 89 MILLION. GERMANY 70 MILLION. GREAT BRITAIN 47 MILLION AND FRANCE 40 MILLION.

In the USSR,

joseph stalin

continued his purge trials, sending millions to death or to Siberia.

Stalin

The airship *hindenburg* landed at Lakehurst, NJ, after the first scheduled transatlantic dirigible flight. Built by the Zeppelin Transport Company, the ship was 804 feet long and 135 feet wide.

BERYL MARKHAM, an English flier, was the first woman to cross the Atlantic alone from east to west. She left Abingdon, England, and crash-landed in a swamp on Camp Breton Island, Nova Scotia. Bad weather forced her to fly blind, relying on her instrument panel.

The first giant panda ever seen in America made its appearance at the San Francisco Zoo.

Sales of automobile trailers peaked at 160,000. Tourist camps for vacationing motorists became hugely popular. Social scientists predicted that soon half the country would be living in trailers.

cultural milestones

The first issue of **LIFE** magazine went on sale in November. **LIFE** was the first magazine to emphasize pictures rather than words. Within six weeks of the first issue, it had more than a million subscribers.

Actor, producer, and director **ORSON WELLES** directed an all-black cast in **MACBETH** for the Negro People's Theatre, part of the Federal Theatre Project.

eugene o'neill

became the first American playwright to win the Nobel Prize for Literature.

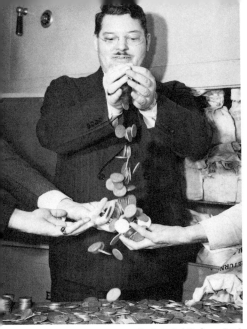

Dr. Craig Earl, "Professor Quiz"

"PROFESSOR QUIZ" was radio's first quiz and give-away program.

A breakthrough special on radio this year was the radio broadcast from Nanking, China, on the occasion of Chiang Kai-shek's kidnapping.

top new programs

1. **"The Kate Smith Show"**
2. **"John's Other Wife,"**
   starring Jimmy Scribner
3. **"The Shadow,"**
   starring Robert Hardy Andrews
4. **"Gangbusters,"**
   starring Phillips H. Lord
5. **"Lux Radio Theatre,"**
   hosted by Cecil B. DeMille
6. **"We, the People,"**
   starring Gabriel Heatter
7. **"Columbia Workshops,"**
   experimental theater
8. **"Chase and Sanborn Hour,"**
   starring Edgar Bergen and Charlie McCarthy
9. **"Professor Quiz,"**
   hosted by Craig Earl
10. **"Pepper Young's Family,"**
    starring Curtis Arnall

All America was reciting

THE SHADOW's

famous intro: "Who knows what evil lurks in the hearts of men? The Shadow knows...."

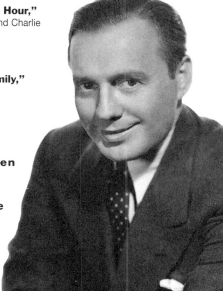

A phony feud began this year between Fred Allen and Jack Benny. The feud started when Allen made fun of Benny's violin playing.

Jack Benny

*Paulette Goddard and
Charlie Chaplin*

milestones

celeb weddings of the year

It was a big year for Hollywood Matrimony, as four mega-couples walked down the aisle.

Paulette Goddard married Charlie Chaplin.

John Barrymore married Elaine Barrie.

Mary Pickford married Buddy Rogers.

Lily Pons married André Kostelanetz.

ACTOR DOUGLAS FAIRBANKS, SR., MARRIED LADY ASHLEY, 32, A ONE-TIME MUSICAL COMEDIENNE, IN PARIS.

DEATHS

Rudyard Kipling,
Nobel Prize-winning author of *The Jungle Book* and *Just So Stories*, died in Burwash, England, January 18.

Anne Sullivan,
who achieved worldwide fame as Helen Keller's teacher, died October 20 in Forest Hills, NY.

Irving J. Thalberg,
the boy wonder head of MGM production under Louis B. Mayer, died September 14 in Santa Monica, CA. He was 37.

Maxim Gorky,
author of *The Lower Depths* and considered the father of Soviet Literature, died June 14 in Moscow.

Ivan Petrovich Pavlov,
the Russian physiologist whose study of conditioned reflexes in dogs won him the Nobel Prize, died in Leningrad, February 27.

Bruno Hauptmann,
the German immigrant convicted of the Lindbergh baby's murder, was executed April 3 in Trenton, NJ.

births

BURT REYNOLDS, film star and first *Cosmopolitan* centerfold, was born February 11 in Waycross, GA.

MARY TYLER MOORE, movie and TV star, was born December 29, in New York City.

ROY ORBISON, legendary moody rocker who recorded "Only the Lonely," was born April 23 in Vernon, TX.

BUDDY HOLLY, fifties rock 'n' roller who fronted the Crickets, was born September 7 in Lubbock, TX.

DALAI LAMA, the 14th Incarnate, exiled Tibetan ruler and religious leader, was born July 6 in Chhija Nangso, Tibet.

36

hit music

1. **the music goes round and round** Tommy Dorsey
2. **the music goes round and round** Riley-Farley Orchestra
3. **moon over miami** Eddy Duchin
4. **alone** Tommy Dorsey
5. **a beautiful lady in blue** Jan Garber
6. **goody-goody** Benny Goodman
7. **lights out** Eddy Duchin
8. **i'm putting all my eggs in one basket** Fred Astaire
9. **it's been so long** Benny Goodman
10. **lost** Guy Lombardo

THE SWING MUSIC CONCERT in New York featured Bob Crosby, Tommy Dorsey, Snuff Smith, Red Norvo, Bunny Berigan, Glen Gray's Casa Loma Orchestra, as well as groups from Paul Whiteman's and Louis Armstrong's bands.

Tommy Dorsey

fred astaire

boasted four top records this year: *Let's Face the Music and Dance, Let Yourself Go, The Way You Look Tonight* and *Pick Yourself Up.*

Fred Astaire

DOWN BEAT's top performers of the year

Benny Goodman—soloist and big band
Ray Noble—"sweet" band
Teddy Wilson—piano
Gene Krupa—drums
Bix Biederbecke—trumpet
Tommy Dorsey—trombone

Cole Porter's score for the Broadway show *Born to Dance* included the hugely popular tune "I've Got You Under My Skin."

the jukebox

became a nationwide phenomenon, present wherever people gathered to listen to music or dance. **Wurlitzer** and **Rock-ola** set the industry standard.

SMALL JAZZ CLUBS SPRANG UP ALL OVER 52ND STREET, IN MANHATTAN, MAKING IT A HOTBED OF HEP. WINGY MALONE HELD COURT AT THE FAMOUS DOOR. SNUFF SMITH AND JONAH JONES WAILED AT THE ONYX.

BENNY GOODMAN STIRRED UP MAJOR CONTROVERSY WHEN HE BECAME THE FIRST BANDLEADER TO RACIALLY INTEGRATE HIS BAND, WITH AFRICAN-AMERICAN MUSICIANS **TEDDY WILSON** ON PIANO AND **LIONEL HAMPTON** ON VIBES.

bestselling

fiction

1. **gone with the wind**
   margaret mitchell

2. **the last puritan**
   george santayana

3. **sparkenbroke**
   charles morgan

4. **drums along the mohawk**
   walter d. edmonds

5. **it can't happen here**
   sinclair lewis

6. **white banners**
   lloyd c. douglas

7. **the hurricane**
   charles nordhoff and
   james norman hall

8. **the thinking reed**
   rebecca west

9. **the doctor**
   mary roberts rinehart

10. **eyeless in gaza**
    aldous huxley

gone with the wind

made publishing history, with sales never before reached by fiction in so short a time. One million copies were sold at a retail price of $3 between June and the end of the year. It was to be the author's only book.

ROBERT FROST WON THE PULITZER THIS YEAR FOR *A FURTHER RANGE.*

That perennial self-help classic, Dale Carnegie's ***HOW TO WIN FRIENDS AND INFLUENCE PEOPLE,*** appeared this year. It contained this famous nugget of wisdom: "Always talk about the other guy."

TWO BASEBALL GREATS MADE THEIR DEBUT THIS YEAR. **JOE DIMAGGIO** PUT ON THE YANKEE UNIFORM. **BOB FELLER** SIGNED ON AS PITCHER FOR THE CLEVELAND INDIANS. FELLER STRUCK OUT 15 IN HIS FIRST GAME.

In boxing, **Max Schmeling** defeated **Joe Louis** in 12 rounds. After the fight, Schmeling spoke of his opponent with contempt: "He fought like an amateur. This is no man who could ever be champion."

In tennis, **FRED PERRY** breezed past Baron Gottfried von Cramm so easily in taking his third straight Wimbledon that fans wondered what was wrong with the German star. **HELEN JACOBS** won her final against Hilda Krahwinkel Sperling, 6–2, 4–6, 7–5.

Baseball Hall of Fame, Cooperstown, NY

the baseball hall of fame

opened this year in Cooperstown, NY. The first players elected were Ty Cobb, Honus Wagner, Babe Ruth, Christy Mathewson, and Walter Johnson.

sports

THE BERLIN OLYMPICS, with Aryan images hanging over the stadium, didn't stop **Jesse Owens,** the Ebony Antelope, from winning 4 gold medals in track and field. Nine out of ten American blacks won gold medals—a complete slap in the face to Adolf Hitler's theories of racial supremacy. Der Führer was so incensed that he left the arena before the awards ceremony.

Jesse Owens

IN AUTO RACING, LOU MEYER WON AN UNPRECEDENTED THIRD VICTORY IN THE INDY 500.

IN HORSE RACING, BOLD VENTURE, RIDDEN BY JOCKEY IRA HANFORD, WON THE KENTUCKY DERBY.

In basketball, the entire **Renaissance Rens** team was voted into the Basketball Hall of Fame. Their overall record was 473–49.

17

The price of a movie this year was 23 cents. Average weekly attendance was 88,000.

notable films

Libeled Lady, directed by Jack Conway, starring Spencer Tracy, Myrna Loy, and Jean Harlow

San Francisco, directed by W. S. Van Dyke, starring Clark Gable and Spencer Tracy

Dodsworth, directed by William Wyler, starring Walter Huston and Ruth Chatterton

Three Smart Girls, directed by Henry Koster, starring Deanna Durbin and Ray Milland

My Man Godfrey, directed by Gregory La Cava, starring Carole Lombard and William Powell

Swing Time, directed by George Stevens, starring Ginger Rogers and Fred Astaire

Camille, directed by George Cukor, starring Greta Garbo and Robert Taylor

TOP BOX-OFFICE STARS THIS YEAR WERE SHIRLEY TEMPLE AND CLARK GABLE.

Clark Gable (left) and Shirley Temple

In **modern times,** Charlie Chaplin's first film in five years, the comic genius stuck to silent pantomime, proving once again that a movie did not need spoken dialogue to be funny or artistic.

Charlie Chaplin, Modern Times

movies

Ronald Colman and Elizabeth Allen starred in the Jack Conway-directed *A Tale of Two Cities.* Shakespeare made a splash on the big screen this year. George Cukor directed Leslie Howard and Norma Shearer in *Romeo and Juliet.*

oscar winners

Best Picture ***The Great Ziegfeld***
Best Actor **Paul Muni,** The Story of Louis Pasteur
Best Actress **Luise Rainer,** The Great Ziegfeld
Best Director **Frank Capra,** Mr. Deeds Goes to Town
Best Screenplay **Pierre Collings** and **Sheridan Gibney,** The Story of Louis Pasteur
The Academy added two new categories this year for supporting players.
Best Supporting Actor **Walter Brennan,** Come and Get It
Best Supporting Actress **Gale Sondergaard,** Anthony Adverse

The VW Beetle made its debut this year. Designed by Ferdinand Porsche, the first Volkswagen ("people's car") rolled off the hand-assembly line on May 26. The first factory to manufacture the vehicle

The year's two big innovations were built-in defrosters and sloping side windows.

cars

36

was inaugurated by Adolf Hitler at Fallerleben, Saxony. The Germans were big admirers of the American automaker Henry Ford. With his Volkswagen, Hitler wanted to emulate Ford by mass-producing a low-priced car.

BUICK CELEBRATED ITS THREE MILLIONTH CAR THIS YEAR.

Cadillac-Fleetwood
TOWN CABRIOLET

Cadillac-Fleetwood Town Cabriolet

Never in the history of the motor car industry has there been another name with the significance of Cadillac-Fleetwood. Everywhere it has come to connote the highest attainment in the motor car builder's art—chassis by Cadillac, body by Fleetwood. For the new Cadillac chassis, Fleetwood has designed and fashioned the finest coachwork it has ever produced. Beautiful, completely luxurious in every detail of fitment and finish, and highly individual in both appearance and form—the new Fleetwood creations stand unique and alone in every aspect of their excellence. Fleetwood builds bodies for the Cadillac Eight, Twelve and Sixteen. The car shown above is the Eight-cylinder Cadillac chassis and the body is the Fleetwood Town Cabriolet. This body is also available on the Twelve-cylinder Cadillac chassis.

KNEE-ACTION • HYDRAULIC BRAKES • CENTER-POINT STEERING • TURRET-TOP TWO-RIDE-STABILIZERS • PEAK-LOAD GENERATOR • TRIPLE-RANGE CHOKE

Hudson introduced a **"radical safety control,"** a steel torque arm that resulted in easier steering and the elimination of nosing down when braking. Also offered on the Hudson was a double automatic emergency braking system with a separate reserve brake system that went into use if the primary brakes failed.

THE AUBURN SPEEDSTER V-12 offered a variety of unique pluses for its price range. Special features of this boat-tailed speedster included a disappearing top, stainless steel outside exhaust pipes, and teardrop fenders—all for $2,245.

'36

fashion

It was anything goes this year in formal wear. Some women opted for short, brightly colored dresses.

FALSIES WERE INTRODUCED ON THE MARKET.

THE SHOE DESIGNER **FERRAGAMO** CAME OUT WITH THE EVENING WEDGE IN GOLD KID AND RED SATIN. ALSO MAKING THEIR APPEARANCE WERE ANKLE BOOTS OF EMBROIDERED FELT OR GOLD KID.

Others went with gold lamé frocks worn with short jackets and pressed pleats. Black silk crepes with white silk overjackets became almost obligatory this season. For daytime wear, tailored wool dresses sporting tight long sleeves and gently bloused bodices were hugely popular.

The bra provided the foundation for the fashionable "high and pointy" look.

A Wardrobe Just as You Want It—That Is the Important Idea Behind This Three-Way Pattern

YOU may not believe in clothes miracles. Neither do we. But literally you can work wonders with a simple pattern like 6789.

First, from this one design you can make all the dresses you need for a short informal vacation. At the left is the casual dress you wear about the cottage in the morning. In the center the same lines made up with a jacket give you an outfit that looks smart anywhere—to the village, at the club. Stretched out below is perfection in a frock designed for sun-basking . . . and, you'll note, for knitting too. That innocent-appearing pocket can be adjusted to suit the size of your yarn ball.

Second, with a pattern as easy to cut out and put together as 6789, you can, with very little effort, have your entire wardrobe just as you want it. You can be sure that each dress fits. You can pick out the most attractive of this season's cottons. You can mix your colors as you please.

Since these dresses are to express your individuality and no one else's, you must be the final judge as to colors and fabrics. But here are a few suggestions:

For the cottage frock, a peasant print—new as a fresh-minted penny, practically impervious to soil. For the village dress, a cool creaseless cotton chiffon under a jacket of linen. And why not choose one of the dark shades that look so striking with a white hat, shoes and bag? We've gone in for bottle green but you may prefer wine or navy. For the sun-back dress, either a rustic linen-like cotton, piqué or that new fabric, sheeting. White is a good color under the sun, but if that is not for you, try a pale pastel. Of course you'll want to add a big-brimmed hat and a pair of beach sandals made of heavy strips of cotton.

Ethel Holland Little
Fashion Editor

6789 Three-way Dress. Sizes, 12 to 20; 30 to 40 bust measures. Size 18 requires 4¼ yards of 35-inch material for cottage version; the same quantity for village version plus 2¾ yards of 35-inch linen for jacket; 4 yards 35-inch material for sun-back version. Price of pattern is 35 cents.

STOP . . . before you discard all those old clothes! Why not change some of them into this year's? Our make-over department will be glad to help. Send all the details plus sketches if you can) and a stamped addressed envelope to Make-over Editor, Woman's Home Companion.

6789

final
factoid

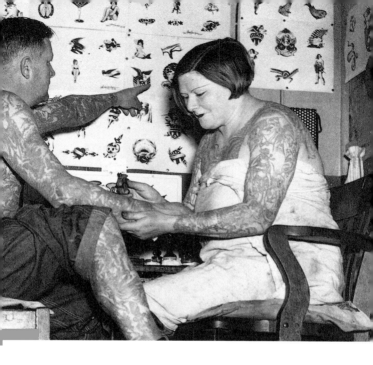

Life magazine reported that one
out of ten Americans sported
tattoos.

archive photos: inside front cover, pages 1, 6, 7, 15, 24, 25, inside back cover

associated press: pages 2, 3, 4, 5, 7, 16, 17

photofest: pages 8, 9, 10, 12, 13, 18, 19

gaslight: pages 21, 23

photo research:
alice albert

coordination:
rustyn birch

design:
carol bokuniewicz design
mutsumi hyuga

'36